LONDON TRANSPORT TRAMS

a black and white album

Robert J Harley

Capital Transport

Front cover Type UCC Feltham car 2104 is pictured in Gray's Inn Road on service 21. The route from Holborn terminus northwards was well suited to these modern vehicles. Peak hour loadings of passengers could be transported quickly and efficiently, as the trams served Kings Cross, Finsbury Park and Wood Green before reaching North Finchley. *LT Museum*

First published 2012

ISBN 978-1-85414-365-5

Published by Capital Transport Publishing Ltd
www.capitaltransport.com

Printed by 1010 International Ltd

Title page London trams had a driving position at each end and therefore could be reversed with a minimum of fuss. The replacing buses and trolleybuses had to find suitable turning places, sometimes in side streets off the main route. This end view of car 1823 at Clapham South Station shows clearly the controller handle to effect braking and to feed power to the motors. The driver's handbrake handle can be seen to the left of the controller. Since the car is operating over conduit track, the trolley pole has been stowed under a roof hook and the trolley rope tied to a cleat in the dash. A fog lamp is fixed to the left of the indicator box. The Venner route 6 stencil can be observed in the top deck end window. *A.B.Cross*

Above Lewisham Clock Tower was a major public transport interchange in the early 1950s. Trams on routes 46 and 72 met those on routes 52, 54 and 58. Former Croydon car 390 heads for Lee High Road, while standard E/1 car 1390 is about to join tracks in Lewisham High Street. The Woolwich and Eltham tram routes lasted until the end of the network. When they were abandoned, traffic was altered to a one-way system round the Clock Tower. *A.J.Watkins*

INTRODUCTION

The London Passenger Transport Board came into existence on Saturday, 1st July 1933. The new organisation took possession of an electric tramway system, the largest in the UK, which consisted of 328 route miles (527km) serviced by 2630 tramcars. The LPTB, quickly christened LONDON TRANSPORT by the public, had its headquarters at 55 Broadway, Westminster, S.W.1. It inherited the task of combining nine municipal operators (London County Council incorporating Leyton, Bexley incorporating Dartford, Croydon, East Ham, Erith, Ilford, Walthamstow and West Ham) with three company owned tramways (Metropolitan Electric, South Metropolitan Electric and London United – also referred to as the Combine tramways).

Earlier casualties that failed to be included in the London Transport network were the entire Dartford fleet, which perished in a depot fire in August 1917, the Barking system replaced by buses in February 1929 and the London United routes in the Kingston and Wimbledon areas, which had been turned over to trolleybus operation.

Tramways within the metropolitan region fulfilled a vital function in transporting millions efficiently and at remarkably low fares. The last LCC route extensions to Grove Park through the Downham Estate and along Westhorne Avenue, Eltham might have given the impression that this form of transport had an assured future; however, after 1933 the policy makers within London Transport thought differently. They soon made it clear that the way forward lay with the trolleybus, a hybrid vehicle tied to overhead wires, but lacking a fixed track in the street. This solution to the alleged obstruction problem posed by tramcars appealed to an increasingly vocal and influential motoring lobby. Modernisation of the existing tramways, as was happening in many European countries, was dismissed as irrelevant to the capital's needs.

It was originally planned to rid London's streets of trams by 1943, but the advent of the Second World War caused a delay in the dismantling of the system, which resulted in diesel buses and not trolleybuses replacing the remaining railbound vehicles. The process was completed by 6th July 1952.

On a technical note it should be pointed out that most of the former LCC lines serving central areas were equipped with the conduit system of power supply. Tramcars were fitted on the underside of the vehicle with a plough device that made electrical contact with T shaped conductor rails encased in a conduit beneath the roadway. Although giving streets a pleasantly uncluttered look, construction costs were so high that, in the interests of economy, routes entering the suburbs and all other tramway operators in London employed the tried and tested trolley pole and overhead wire method of current collection.

Included in this album are several official views; my thanks go to the London Transport Museum for permission to use them. As the abandonment programme began in earnest, amateur tram enthusiasts took up their cameras to record scenes which were rapidly disappearing from the streets. We owe a debt of gratitude to these individuals, whose pictures, published in this album, have preserved an urban way of life now gone for good. Ironically, many of these aficionados who considered themselves inspired visionaries – prophets unacknowledged in their own land – were castigated by professional transport men and town planners as cranks and eccentrics. However, their dream of a modern, environmentally friendly tramway system as a solution to traffic congestion became reality with the opening of Croydon Tramlink in 2000. Trams were to be seen once more on the streets.

Inevitably, some pictures taken in the late 1940s and early 1950s depict a city 'knocked about a bit' by the recent depredations of wartime bombing raids. When the sun did shine, photographers such as John Meredith and Don Thompson were on hand to capture the moment. The world of small local shops, suburban houses with walled front gardens, British built motor cars and smartly dressed folk, many wearing a hat, comes alive with the trams playing a vital part.

That the trams continued for as long as they did is a tribute to the men and women who worked on them and maintained them. In its last years the tramway system acquired an almost mythical status among those who suspected, quite rightly, that the era of cheap fares would cease, when buses took over. Whatever the weather, the trams could be guaranteed to keep running. Londoners relied on the railbound vehicles to transport them slowly but surely in the winter fogs that often blanketed the capital. After the trams had gone, exhaust gases from the replacing diesel buses were considered a contributory factor in the infamous 'killer smog' of December 1952.

In assembling material for this album I have tried to place vehicles in class order with reference to their original owners. Since LCC vehicles formed the bulk of the post 1933 fleet, they claim the lion's share of the pictures in the second half of the album. We start by looking at the rolling stock acquired from the London area municipal systems, plus those vehicles from the three Combine tramways. Bearing in mind London transport inherited a motley collection of trams in varying states of repair; it should not be a surprise that some cars did not survive long enough to receive a new fleet number. It should also be borne in mind that the Combine company owned tramways (LUT, MET & SMET) divided their trams into **types**, unlike the LCC and some other municipal systems which grouped their vehicles into **classes**. Strangely, this odd distinction was perpetuated by London Transport.

My gratitude goes especially to Dave Jones of the LCC Tramways Trust and to Jim Whiting of Capital Transport for their valuable assistance in preparing this album. I also wish to give an honourable mention to my fellow enthusiasts, past and present: J.Bonell, W.A.Camwell, C.Carter, A.B.Cross, Gerald Druce, R.Elliott, J.C.Gillham, C.F.Klapper, A.D.Packer, J.H.Price, H.B.Priestley, N.Rayfield, F.G.Reynolds, G.N.Southerden, D.Voice, A.J.Watkins, H.Wightman, J.Wills and R.J.S.Wiseman.

Arguably London's most distinguished tramway enthusiast, Sir John Betjeman, Poet Laureate and connoisseur of route 7 from Parliament Hill Fields to Kings Cross and Holborn, penned the following lines..

On roaring iron down the Holloway Road
The red trams and the brown trams pour...

With these words in mind let our journey commence..

Robert J Harley   July 2012

We begin our journey in North Kent at Bexleyheath Broadway on a rainy day in the summer of 1933. Now well past their prime, cars 26C and 30C of the former Bexley fleet observe the time honoured ritual of waiting for one another at a passing loop. In the autumn these vehicles, original members of LCC class B, will be towed away for scrap and the Woolwich to Dartford route will become a high priority for trolleybus conversion. *G.N.Southerden*

Whilst Bexley trams received a C suffix, those at Erith boasted the letter D. Car 11D dated from 1905. Depicted almost thirty years later in its new London Transport livery, it still looks good for a few miles yet. However, the powers-that-be decided that open balcony, single truck trams did not present the right image for the capital city. This vehicle was scrapped in February 1936. *G.N.Southerden*

Three former Eastenders meet at Well Hall Circus, Eltham. Leading car 86 from East Ham passes ex Leyton E/3 class car 203. Meanwhile in the background an ex West Ham vehicle appears to have dewired at the roundabout. *D.A.Thompson/LCCT Trust*

In between the summer showers an ex East Ham car is seen outside Abbey Wood Depot. The building was constructed by the LCC in 1910. In London Transport days it had a maximum capacity of 86 trams, although in practice this figure was never reached. Converted to a bus garage in 1952, it has subsequently been demolished. *A.J.Watkins*

East Ham bogie car 83 proved a good investment and after service in East London it was transferred south of the Thames to Abbey Wood Depot. Here it is seen making its way through the trees bordering Eltham Road, east of Lee Green. Note the 1952 fashions of the cyclists on their 'racing' bikes and the young family who have just left the tram. *A.D.Packer*

In the Mile End Road, near the crossing with tram route 77 at Grove Road and Burdett Road, the conductor of an Ilford bound tram perches on the rear fender in order to put up the trolley in advance of the change pit from conduit to overhead. Passengers take this opportunity to disembark from the former East Ham vehicle, before it follows the ex Leyton E/3 tram across the road junction.
LT Museum

Shortly after this view was taken in July 1952, the trams departed, leaving Southern Region's trains to carry the electric traction banner. This location has changed in the intervening years. Eltham Well Hall Station was replaced, relocated and renamed in response to engineering works that projected the Rochester Way Relief Road under the roadway where car 100 is standing. According to local legend the tram tracks under the railway bridge were never pulled up and they now reside beneath the road surface. *D.A.Thompson/LCCT Trust*

The London County Council operated tramways in Leyton on behalf of the local authority. Leyton E/3 class car 167 of 1931 is pictured on Falcon Road, Battersea. Although the highway is wide enough for passenger loading islands, no modernisation funds could be found for the 'obsolete' tramways. The trolleybus wires were used as a connecting link between route 612 and the 626/628/655 terminus at Grant Road, Clapham Junction. *D.A.Thompson/LCCT Trust*

Tram route 34 on its journey from Kings Road, Chelsea to Blackfriars probably tackled more right angle bends than any other service. Here at the Princes Head, Battersea, car 167 makes the turn into Falcon Road. Notice there was still plenty of time in those days for pedestrians to saunter across the main road without fear of being run over. Above them all are the trolleybus wires used by route 612. It perished with tram route 34 on 30th September 1950. *D.A. Thompson/LCCT Trust*

On Norwood Road by Trinity Rise there was a section of single track, where the carriageway narrowed. Car 173 is working route 33 to Manor House via the Kingsway Subway. Note the TRAM PINCH warning sign for motorists, as the rails came closer to the kerb by the tree lined Brockwell Park. *D.A.Thompson/LCCT Trust*

After the Second World War the remaining trams in North London on Kingsway Subway routes 31, 33 and 35 had to share road space with the trolleybuses. At the corner of Rosebery Avenue and St John Street car 170 heads northwards to Islington Green. The sturdily built E/3 class cars, both of the Leyton and LCC variety, provided the mainstay of the Kingsway Subway services. *D.A.Thompson/LCCT Trust*

There seems to be some trouble with the points at Manor House terminus. Car 1947 waits for the permanent way department to fix the problem before departing southwards. Car 185 has lost its original Alpax metal windscreen and now sports a less attractive wooden one, courtesy of Charlton Repair Works. *D.A.Thompson/LCCT Trust*

The lady about to board car 186 has the opportunity to pass the time of the day with the conductor. Although London trams were often accused of obstructing the carriageway, there appears to be little evidence here of any other traffic. Note the combined trolleybus and tram stop attached to traction standard 543.

Most of the Leyton E/3 trams saw service until the end of the system in July 1952. Pursued by a British Road Services lorry, car 186 heads along the Old Kent Road. Note the small shops and the marvellous collection of 1950s road vehicles. Parking wasn't a problem in those days. *D.A.Thompson/LCCT Trust*

Car 202 is depicted in Streatham High Road at St Leonard's Church junction. The date is 1st October 1950 and over in the Battersea and Wandsworth areas the first stage of London's post-war tramway abandonment scheme has just taken place. Car 202 has been transferred from Wandsworth Depot and is now doing service on route 8. This vehicle was scrapped in May 1952. *J.H.Meredith*

Many Londoners used to take advantage of cheap fares to spend a summer Sunday exploring Epping Forest. A world away from the grime of the city, car 203, depicted on home territory, pauses on the private right of way at the side of Whipps Cross Road adjacent to the forest. Photographer Don Thompson captured this attractive scene in the last peacetime summer, before the Royal Navy required his services in defence of the realm. *D.A.Thompson/ LCCT Trust*

Sunblinds have been unfurled at the junction of Brockley Rise and Stanstead Road, Catford. The motorman of car 204 has left his charge in order to speak to an inspector. Meanwhile car 580 heads into town via New Cross. Traffic lights at this road intersection seem an unnecessary extravagance. *D.A.Thompson/LCCT Trust*

The Boleyn public house stands at the junction of Green Street and Barking Road. Former West Ham car 291 is working local service 1A and is about to return to Stratford Broadway. In the pre-war period football crowds attending the nearby Upton Park ground could be efficiently shifted by lines of trams stabled on these tracks. *H.Wightman*

There is no need for ten shilling lightweight macks on this fine sunny day at Ilford. Former West Ham car 305 is seen in pre-war condition, while working route 63. Because of their lower than normal mouldings on the upper deck side panels, these vehicles were provided with resized advertisements. This route was converted to trolleybuses on 5th November 1939, when lighting fires for Guy Fawkes was strictly forbidden due to wartime blackout restrictions. Bow Depot was closed to trams and car 305 went south of the Thames, eventually ending up at Abbey Wood Depot. *D.A. Thompson/LCCT Trust*

Beresford Square, Woolwich was a major tramway interchange. In the last week of the system former West Ham car 312 loads passengers for the short trip to Eltham on service 44. Shoppers and market traders fill a busy scene. Note the imposing gateway of the Royal Arsenal in the background. The lone motor vehicle looks very out of place.
C.Carter

The bulk of the London Transport fleet was composed of eight wheel (bogie) cars. This scene in Croydon on the Thornton Heath route illustrates how car 373 could shift large numbers of rush hour passengers. Men clamber up the stairs to the top deck, where smoking was allowed. Mothers with small children would normally make a bee line for a seat in the lower saloon. The conductor was on hand to see that his 'load' was on board, before signalling to the motorman to start the car.
C.F.Klapper/Omnibus Society

19

66
FOREST HILL
via BROCKLEY & NEW
375
NEV 841
E.F.HASLING & SON
BISTO
GOLD FLAKE
CAPSTAN

Route 42 to Thornton Heath was the last traditional single track and loops layout in London. In spite of the apparent handicap of one tram having to wait for another, as illustrated here with cars 385 and 375, the line was one of the most profitable on the post-war system. The leisurely ride along Brigstock Road obviously appealed to the locals.

London Road, Broad Green, Croydon is the setting for this view of car 381. Evidence of bomb damage can be seen at the corner of St James's Road. When this picture was taken in January 1951, vacant sites, destroyed in the recent conflict, were often concealed behind advertisement hoardings. Trams at this location have only another few weeks to run, before they are replaced by buses on 7th April. *J.H.Meredith*

Opposite Former Croydon car 375 was fitted with windscreens in July 1939. On 29th September 1951, it is depicted negotiating track work repairs in Brockley Road. The permanent way gang have stacked granite setts on the pavement so that they can gain unrestricted access to the running rails. Note the boy dressed in school uniform and the gentleman in the wheelchair, who is collecting money for a flag day. *J.H.Meredith*

Waterloo Station tram terminus was served by route 68. It was a handy transfer point for passengers taking the train to Southampton, Bournemouth and the West Country. However, it was well short of main traffic objectives across the River Thames in central London. Former Croydon car 387 waits to return southwards to Greenwich. The track layout here was originally configured for trailer operation. *D.A.Thompson/LCCT Trust*

22

Ex Croydon car 380 was renovated by London Transport in November 1936 and lasted until January 1952. It is seen here at the junction of London Road and Station Road, West Croydon, where trolleybus routes 630 and 654 crossed tram routes 16, 18 and local service 42. After an absence of many decades trams have returned to this location in the form of Croydon Tramlink. *D.Simpson*

Car 2046 was originally numbered 57 in the Walthamstow fleet. It was scrapped in February 1952. In happier days it is depicted on tracks in Downham Way, constructed by the LCC to serve a new housing estate. The overhead wires on this stretch were configured to accept bow and pantograph current collectors. This was part of an experiment carried out in 1933 to reduce dewirements from the conventional trolley pole. Needless to say, the new owners, London Transport showed no interest in furthering the tests. *D.A. Thompson/LCCT Trust*

This view of a convoy of trams awaiting return to New Cross Depot was meat and drink to the opponents of the railbound vehicles. There were probably just over twenty trams in this line up. New Cross was London's largest tram depot and this traffic bottleneck could have been alleviated by constructing an extra access track to the car sheds, but such a solution was never to be implemented.

Arguably London's most stylish trams were the Felthams. Officially designated type UCC, they hailed from the London United and Metropolitan Electric systems. In the early 1930s they brought a touch of streamlined luxury to travellers more accustomed to wooden seats and the angular style of the traditional London tram. Car 2080 is edging out of Wood Green Depot. Watching the departure is a small group of lads, who are probably interested in the building work necessary to house trolleybuses. Wood Green began life as a horse tram depot and it still survives, although the trolleybuses were replaced by diesel buses in 1961.

Three distinct tramcar types greet the photographer as he surveys the scene at Wood Green Depot. Former Metropolitan Electric cars 2294 and single decker 2303 face imminent extinction. The Felthams will be transferred south of the river to Streatham, where they will take up service on the local routes plus the trunk service to Croydon and Purley.
W.A.Camwell

Feltham car 2102 has encountered some difficulty and is being shunted by a breakdown tender. The location is the Vauxhall gyratory system outside the offices of Dalton's Weekly. At peak times around 270 trams an hour passed this spot, so it was imperative that the obstruction was moved as quickly as possible. Although black blank displays were included on some London Transport tram blinds, they were very rarely used. *A.J.Watkins*

The location is Streatham High Road at the county boundary between London and Surrey. Car 2123's original home was on the long London United route 7 from Shepherds Bush to Uxbridge. Then it bore the LUT fleet number 354. After being sold by London Transport to Leeds, it was subsequently numbered 564; it finally ended up as the Yorkshire city's number 557. *J.H.Meredith*

Routes 8 and 20 terminated at the end of the pedestrian safety refuge at Victoria. Further along on the second loading island cars working services 54, 58 and 66 could be boarded. We observe Little Ben clock tower in the background, while nearer to us the motorman of Feltham 2136 adjusts his driving mirror ready for departure. These large tramcars offered the traveller a warm and cosy ride home, when it was raining cats and dogs outside.

Passengers face a choice of public transport at the stop by the theatre in Streatham Hill. The date is 15th June 1949 and Feltham 2126 is about to set off to Victoria Embankment via Kennington and Westminster. Loading islands were not a regular feature of London tramway operation. Their widespread introduction could have saved many lives in road accidents caused by careless motorists striking people, who were attempting to board or alight at tram stops. *J.H.Meredith*

The Felthams always seemed to dominate the available road space. Here in Balham High Road car 2124 will probably soon catch up to the standard E/1 tram ahead of it. The shop on the right is selling a wonderful array of British made bicycles. Prices start at a modest thirty shillings (£1.50)! *D.A.Thompson/LCCT Trust*

Many streets in South London were of sufficient width to have segregated tram tracks. Such a modernisation policy was not on the agenda of London Transport. It takes but little imagination to picture Feltham car 2150 on a more up-to-date track layout.

Archaic regulations meant that open fronted trams were a common sight on the streets of 1930s London. Originally numbered 253 in the Metropolitan Electric Tramways fleet, type H car 2185 is depicted in Kings Cross at the junction of Grays Inn Road and Caledonian Road. These vehicles with their distinctive six side window lower decks perished in the pre-war trolleybus conversion programme.

Opposite Car 2167 was one of the prototype Feltham trams. Constructed in 1929 and originally numbered 330 in the Metropolitan Electric fleet, this vehicle acted as a test bed for the forthcoming production batch. Depicted in Streatham High Road, car 2167 was scrapped at Purley Depot in December 1949. The reason given for its early demise was that it was 'non standard'. *J.H.Meredith*

Car 2276 was another MET vehicle that was broken up prematurely. It was originally type G car 231 and had been modernised with the installation of driver's windscreens. It is seen here at the tram station in North Finchley, which was opened fully in February 1935 and had a remarkably short life, being closed to trams in March 1938. The location was then used by the replacing trolleybuses.

A gentleman in fashionable 1930s cycling attire looks past car 2308 (former MET type E car 140) as it moves sedately along Buckingham Road, Wood Green. In the London Transport era single deck trams were a rarity. The two Alexandra Palace routes perished on 23rd February 1938; car 2308, with its open driving platforms, polished brass fittings and immaculate red and off white livery, then disappeared in favour of a motor bus.

Former London United trunk route 7 to Uxbridge was worked by a combination of Feltham and type T vehicles, such as car 312, seen here at Southall Pump. This tram is depicted in the late summer of 1933 before it was repainted and renumbered 2328 in the LT fleet. Route 7 was one of the network's best earners, but this economic success did not prevent conversion to trolleybuses on 15th November 1936. *C.Carter*

Shepherds Bush terminus was the nearest the trams got to potentially more lucrative traffic objectives in the West End. Car 2406 is a former London United vehicle of type T. When they first appeared in 1905, these trams were considered the height of luxury, thus earning them the nickname of 'palace cars'. Now long past its heyday, this vehicle awaits its fate at the hands of trolleybus route 657 to Hounslow.

The bulk of the London Transport fleet consisted of vehicles acquired from the London County Council. The E/1 class tram, of which there were over a thousand built between 1907 and 1930, represented the 'standard model'. It incorporated design features from the earlier E class vehicles. It has to be said that by the 1930s the 'standard model' with open platforms appeared distinctly old fashioned. All members of the E/1 class inherited by London Transport in 1933 were equipped for conduit and overhead trolley operation. Car 1025 was preserved and now belongs to the large vehicle collection of the London Transport Museum. In this view at the Hampstead Heath terminus, car 552, accompanied by a motor bus, has just emerged from the one way section of Fleet Road. E class car 537 leads the procession in the other direction towards Constantine Road and Agincourt Road. Trolleybus overhead has already been erected and trams will disappear on 10th July 1938 from the terminus. All E class trams were scrapped by the beginning of 1939; the only escapee was car 420, which was renumbered 1597 and reclassified E/1.

Pictured in the early days of the London Passenger Transport Board, this E class tram on service 30 to Tooting Junction pauses at the change pit in Putney Bridge Road, Wandsworth. An attendant forks the conduit plough underneath the car, while the conductor stands ready to pull down the trolley pole. This regular process of changing the method of current collection was performed many hundreds of times a day all over London. As regards the 1933 fashion scene, just about everyone in this view was smartly turned out; in those days hats were de rigueur.

Evidence of the 1920s and 1930s building boom that created 'semi detached suburbia' is apparent in the background to this view of E/1 class car 837 at Eltham Green. In spite of London Transport's intention to dismantle the tram system, investment in new track relocations did take place. In May 1935 work started on a roundabout at the Yorkshire Grey junction of Eltham Road and Westhorne Avenue. Note the permanent way gang installing a crossover for short working trams. After the war this was used as the terminus of route 44. *G.N.Southerden*

At the Bakers Arms, Leyton on a warm day in the summer of 1938 we are treated to a veritable cornucopia of vintage transport. On Sunday afternoons it was possible to take a route 31 tram from Garratt Lane, Tooting via the Kingsway Subway to Leyton. Car 907 is proceeding past the route 31 terminus to the end of the line at Woodford. The curves connecting Lea Bridge Road with the High Street have already been severed; the whole tramway infrastructure at this location will be abandoned on 11th June 1939. *H.B.Priestley*

Pride of the system, car 1 was the prototype of a planned new fleet of trams that unfortunately never materialised. Built by the LCC, it entered service in 1932 adorned in a striking blue and cream paint scheme, thus earning it the nickname of 'Bluebird'. Here it is seen in London Transport livery, whilst working service 10 from Southwark Bridge to Tooting Broadway. It was sold to Leeds in 1951 and now resides awaiting full restoration in the National Tramway Museum at Crich. *LCCT Trust*

Car 978 was reconditioned by London Transport in March 1936 and was withdrawn in January 1951. In this pre-war view on the Embankment, it is about to work an all night service to Downham. The journey was timed at 48 minutes. *LT Museum*

The traffic queue waiting for the lights to change at the 'Unicorn' junction of Norton Folgate and Great Eastern Street features cars 1069 and 567, plus a splendid assortment of petrol driven vehicles including a taxi and two buses. Traction standards, erected in the summer of 1938 in preparation for the new trolleybus overhead, indicate that the days of the trams at this location are numbered. Service 49 ceased on 5th February 1939 to be followed on 11th June by the 57 to Leyton. *H.B.Priestley*

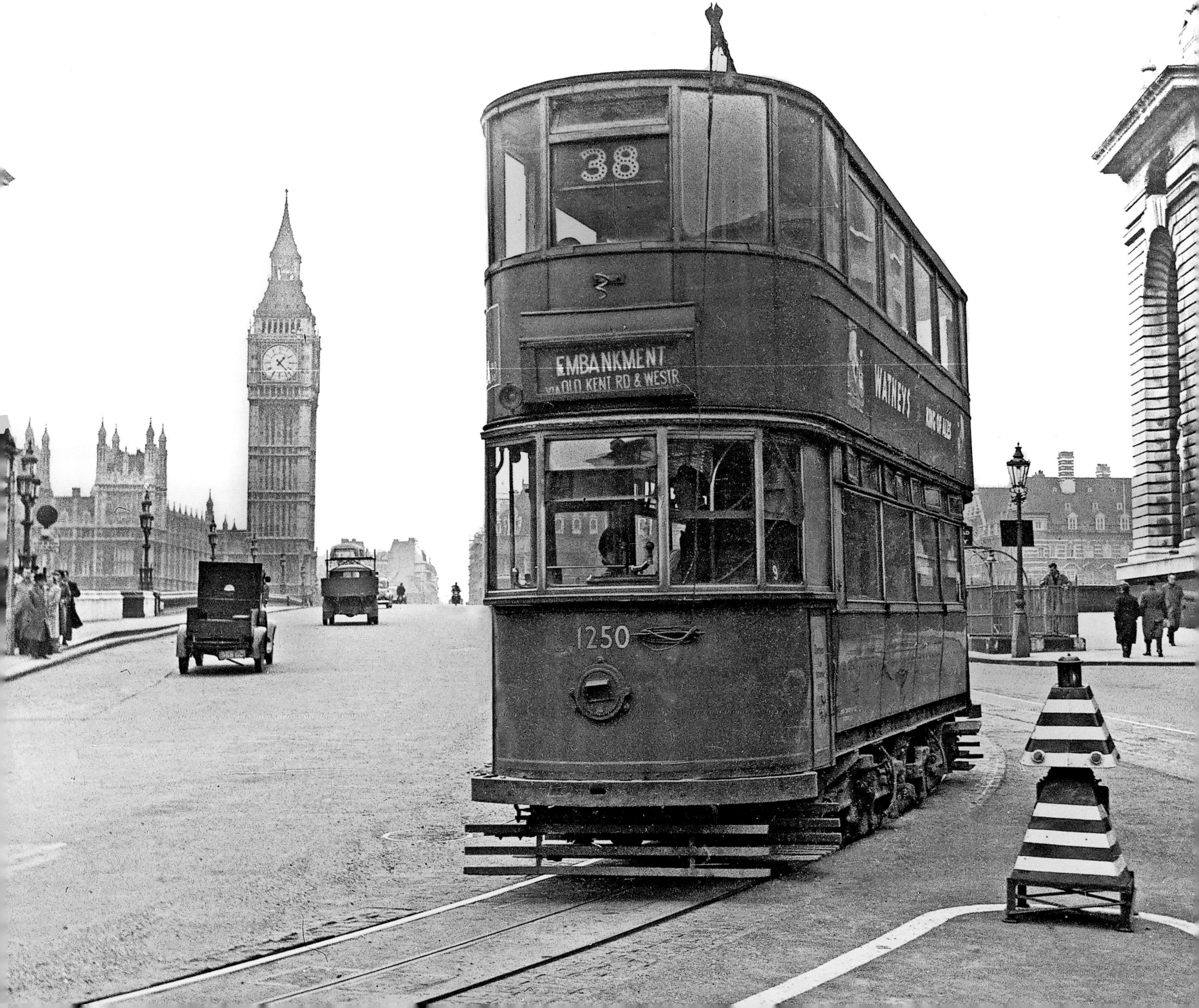
38
EMBANKMENT
VIA OLD KENT RD & WESTR
WATNEYS
1250

Motorman and Conductor pose in the summer sunshine of 1940, as car 1322 waits to return to Barking Broadway. This peaceful scene conceals the fact that on the other side of the English Channel Allied troops were fighting a losing battle against the Wehrmacht. In wartime trams became a precious commodity; therefore car 1322 avoided the scrapheap and was later sent for further service in South London. Note the first type of blackout mask. *P.Broadley/LCCT Trust*

Opposite Car 1250 is beginning to show its age as it rounds the curve on to Westminster Bridge. Note the 'revised' style of blackout headlight mask found on all the post-war fleet. In one rather facetious reply to an enquiry an LT official suggested that the masks had not been removed because street lighting on tram routes was good and, besides, since the vehicle ran on rails the tram driver knew where he was going in the dark! *J.H.Meredith*

A solidly built terrace of houses forms the background to this view of car 1325 on the East India Dock Road. Two slip boards advertise the Shilling All Day Ticket, which gave Londoners the freedom to explore the tram and trolleybus system for the equivalent of today's fivepence piece. This tram was scrapped at Hampstead Depot in April 1939. Route 65 was converted to trolleybuses on 9th June 1940.

Car 1406 had screens fitted in March 1938 and it was scrapped at Penhall Road, Charlton in January 1952. Passengers alighting from Southern Region and London Underground electric trains at the nearby New Cross Gate Station could transfer directly to one of the many tram services using New Cross Road. On this fine day, over six decades ago, people have turned out dressed in their summer best. *D.A.Thompson/LCCT Trust*

Opposite In a characteristic pose the motorman of car 1486 employs his point iron to switch tracks at Vauxhall Cross. Trams followed the rest of the traffic in a large one way scheme inaugurated in May 1938. In normal service this task would be carried out by a pointsman stationed in front of a small canvas hut on the pavement. Perhaps the chap was off work that day or more probably the points were playing up. Automatic points worked on the power and coast principle were a rarity on the system. *J.H.Meredith*

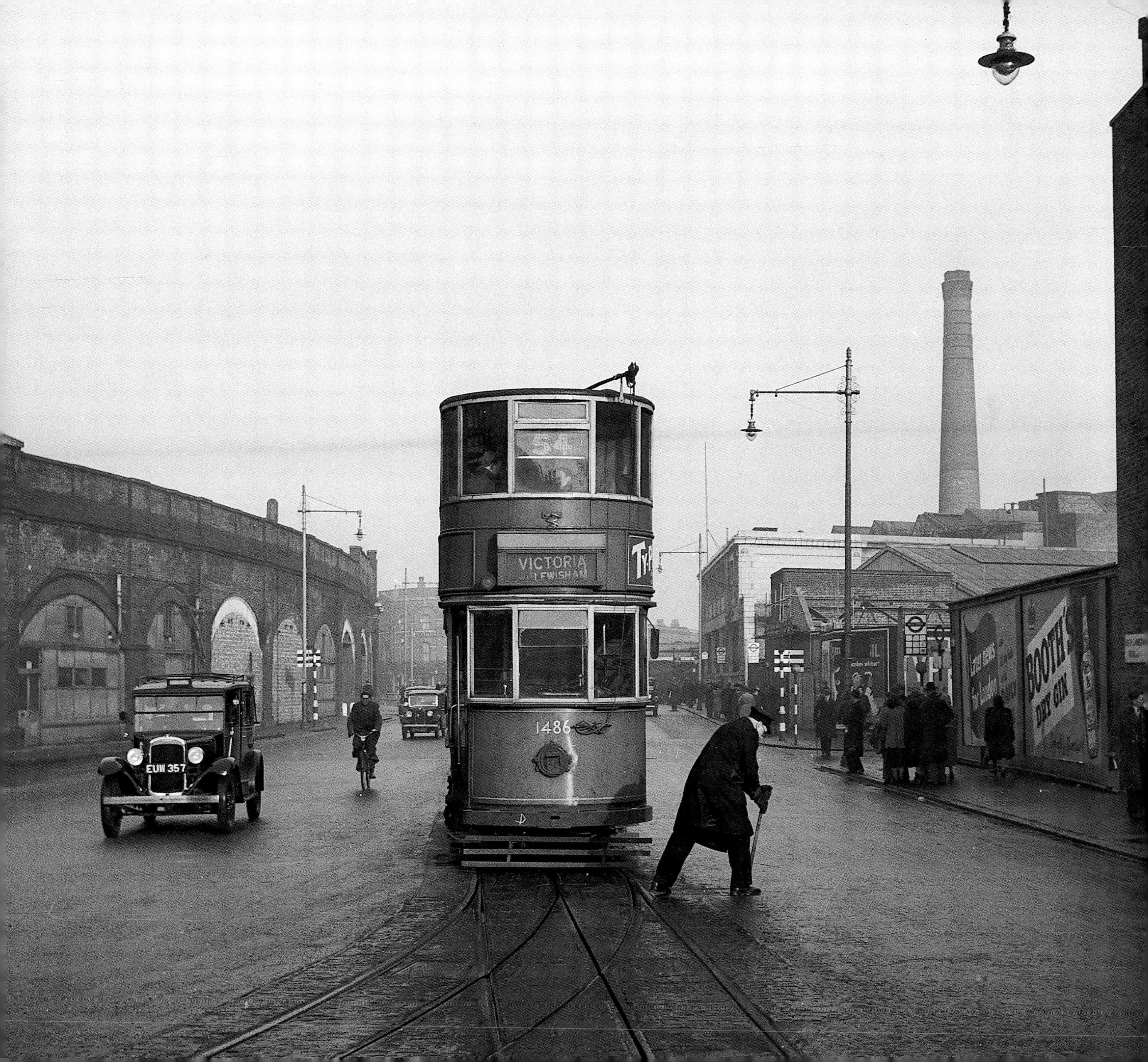
VICTORIA
LEWISHAM
1486
EUW 357
BOOTH'S
DRY GIN

Above The leafy tranquillity of suburban Catford echoes to the sound of traction motors, as car 1598 slows for the crossover on Stanstead Road by Beechfield Road. Route 74 succumbed to bus route 179 on 6th January 1952. This apparently idyllic scene has since been drastically altered by a vast increase of motor traffic coupled with a miasma of exhaust fumes. *D.A.Thompson/LCCT Trust*

Left Shoppers are out in force in Tooting Broadway as the motorman of car 1596 carefully pilots his charge through the throng of people. On the indicator box of this vehicle can be seen the remnants of the three colour light system used to identify services before the introduction by the LCC of route numbers. Even numbers were applied to services south of the Thames, odd numbers to those terminating north of the river and to Kingsway Subway routes.

Car 1658 has been curtailed on its route to Grove Park and has now been directed to terminate at Downham, Bromley Road. Unlike their central bus colleagues, tramway and trolleybus staff had more flexible working arrangements and it was quite common to work several different routes on one shift. *J.Wills*

Prefabs were a feature of post-war British life. This form of 'temporary' accommodation can be glimpsed behind the trees on Clapham Common. Car 1783 pauses at the stop by Lynette Avenue in August 1950. Again, it is amazing that this main trunk road has so little traffic that those seeking to board the tram don't have to take their lives in their hands when they step off the pavement.

47

Depicted on the curve from Downham Way into Bromley Road, car 54 is depot bound for New Cross Gate. Just behind the photographer is a change pit from conduit to overhead for the last section to the terminus at Grove Park. The parade of suburban shops is typical of an era before large scale chain stores, supermarkets and out of town malls. The costumier and milliner no doubt attracted the stylish ladies of the Metropolitan Borough of Lewisham with the latest 1950 fashion creations. *D.A.Thompson/LCCT Trust*

The configuration of the track in Merton Road, Wimbledon, owed much to the old London United company. Car 1797 enters the Pelham Road loop. The trolley head will soon pass under a contact in the overhead that will alter the signal on the traction standard to two diagonal lights, thus indicating a clear road for trams proceeding towards Wimbledon terminus. *J.H.Meredith*

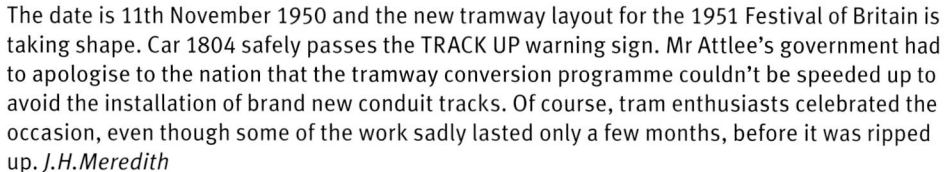

The date is 11th November 1950 and the new tramway layout for the 1951 Festival of Britain is taking shape. Car 1804 safely passes the TRACK UP warning sign. Mr Attlee's government had to apologise to the nation that the tramway conversion programme couldn't be speeded up to avoid the installation of brand new conduit tracks. Of course, tram enthusiasts celebrated the occasion, even though some of the work sadly lasted only a few months, before it was ripped up. *J.H.Meredith*

The lower deck interior of E/1 car 1778 was furnished in a strictly functional way and was typical of most of the fleet. Moquette covered seats had backs that could be flipped over according to the direction of travel. In rush hours those unfortunate enough not to get a seat had to steady themselves by 'strap hanging'. The door separating the motorman from the passengers was usually closed during the journey.

In Wandsworth Road at the junction with Nine Elms Lane car 1809 rumbles over the crossover opposite Miles Street. Note that this vehicle has metal bracing straps hold the car body square, so loose were the main body joints. This make do and mend programme temporarily prolonged the life of the oldest rolling stock. Of course, official policy would not countenance the construction of new vehicles. The date is 6th August 1950 and the straps will have to maintain structural integrity until the car is scrapped in October 1951.
J.H.Meredith

Under the trolleybus wires at Tooting Broadway we observe cars 1819 and 1787. Former tram service 30 crossed here, until it was replaced by trolleybus route 630 in September 1937. On 11th November 1950, when this view was taken, the first stage of the post-war abandonment scheme had already taken place. Route 2 would breathe its last symbolically at stage two on 7th January 1951. *J.H.Meredith*

28
CLAPHAM
JUNCTION
1824
NEW
LONDON
EDITION
for later news
and all the facts
DAILY MAIL
Making new friends EVERY DAY
ARMY
STOP

The end of the line at Wimbledon Town Hall was a purpose built terminus outside the main traffic stream. It was also the interchange point with trolleybus routes 604 and 605 to Hampton Court and Twickenham. The drivers of standard E/1 cars 1846 and 1777 await instructions from the assembled multitude of LT inspectors.

Opposite After picking up his load of passengers the driver of car 1824 will have to check that the points ahead of him are correctly set for Wandsworth Road and not Nine Elms Lane. This scene illustrates the potential for accidental injury to people waiting for a tram. In 1950, unlike the highway code in continental European countries, there was no British statute to require motorists to stop to allow passengers to board or alight. *J.H.Meredith*

Car 1849 is passing the imposing frontage of County Hall in York Road, Lambeth. It is about to turn into Addington Street. These tracks were opened on 11th June 1950. Preparations for the 1951 Festival of Britain on the South Bank can be seen in the background.

To an untrained observer all London's post-war trams, with the exception of the Felthams, looked alike. The leading E/1 car in this view at Eltham Green has its first two fleet digits obscured. It is followed by ex East Ham car 93. At the rear is a rehab E/1 tram, which could be immediately recognised by the flat lower deck sides. It lacked the traditional waist and rocker panels of the two vehicles ahead of it.
F.G.Reynolds/LCCT Trust

The '500' series of class E/1 was constructed in 1930 utilising the trucks and equipments of scrapped class F and G single deck trams. They were painfully slow vehicles and crews from New Cross Depot nicknamed them snails, tortoises or slow coaches. They could often be found on dockland routes 68 and 70. Here at London Bridge, Tooley Street terminus we observe cars 555 and 586. *J.H.Meredith*

The enforced rebuilding of Creek Bridge, Deptford was yet another embarrassment for London Transport. New conduit tracks on the lifting bridge were fully opened on 30th July 1949. Cars 584 and 1170 await the right of way. After all this investment the whole lot was junked on 10th July 1951, when diesel buses replaced tram routes 68 and 70. *J.H.Meredith*

Pollarded Plane trees line McLeod Road, Abbey Wood, as car 565 slowly negotiates the curve into Basildon Road on the climb towards Plumstead. The road here was wide enough for trolleybuses on route 698 to pass tramcars, hence the impressive overhead wire layout. In the centre of the picture the tram and trolleybus stop sign was illuminated by gas light after dark. *D.A. Thompson/LCCT Trust*

The two dockland routes 68 and 70 had a character all of their own. They played a part in the 1951 British film *Pool of London*. Here in Jamaica Road car 594 is about to enter the single track by Drummond Road. Note the spotless condition of this tramcar and the wonderfully ornate, early electric street lamp. *J.H.Meredith*

Car 595 is working from New Cross Depot and is heading along Deptford Broadway in the direction of Greenwich Church. Cinema goers often used the trams in South London. Before the lure of TV took hold, watching the silver screen was one of the most popular leisure activities. The Gaumont poster is advertising the Hollywood film *You're in the Navy Now*, starring Gary Cooper and Jane Greer. It was one of the top box office hits of 1951. *J.H.Meredith*

The 1930 batch of E/1 trams could always be recognised by the thicker middle window frame on the lower deck. Car 601 has found its final home on service 46. It didn't quite last until the end of the system. It was scrapped in June 1952. *R.Hubble/LCCT Trust*

The rehab or renovated E/1 trams were a sort of halfway house between traditional and modern. Car 984 received its rejuvenation treatment in September 1936. It is seen on Bromley Road, Bellingham by Randlesdown Road crossover. Most windows and both bulkhead doors are open due to the warm weather on 27th August 1949.

In the autumn of 1934 work started on car 1038 as part of a programme to recondition some of the former LCC E/1 class cars, of which there were 1050 on the books. As can be seen from this picture, the staff at Charlton Works did a creditable job, bearing in mind the lack of motivation to create a more modern look, when the future of the tramways looked so bleak. In the event, 150 vehicles were treated. An example of the species – car 1622 – can be seen at the National Tramway Museum in Crich, Derbyshire. *LT Museum*

A double helping of rehabs is on offer at Grove Park terminus. Cars 1310 and 1491 supply cheap and frequent transport from the suburbs into central London. They were also ideal for shopping trips to the large department stores in Lewisham. *J.H.Meredith*

Car 1387 got the rehab treatment in July 1936. It is depicted on Norwood Road, Herne Hill. The motorman has just shut off power as the tram is about to pass under a section power feed to the overhead wires. Electric current was supplied to the tramways at approximately half a mile intervals. At this location there were automatic points on the tracks leading to central London. *J.H.Meredith*

The Dun Cow, 279 Old Kent Road was a well known local hostelry in the tram era. Rehab car 1619 passes on a short working to nearby Bricklayers Arms. The chap on his drop handlebar bike reminds us that in those days cyclists knew to cross tramlines at an oblique angle, thus avoiding a nasty spill. However, granite setts still presented a challenge, as they were notoriously slippery in wet weather. After the trams ceased the rails were lifted and the carriageway was resurfaced in asphalt. *D.A.Thompson/LCCT Trust*

Arguably the most versatile of the four wheel cars inherited by London Transport were the members of the M class. Former LCC car 1705 has been drafted across the county boundary into Kent to work the service from Woolwich, Beresford Square to Dartford, Horns Cross. In 1934 this route was given the number 96 which lives on today as the bus route linking the two towns. An adult fare of eight old pence (3p) covered the whole distance in a journey time of 76 minutes. This tram, pictured outside the original Bexley Council depot in Bexleyheath, has yet to receive the well known LONDON TRANSPORT fleet name, which was applied to vehicles from 1934 onwards. *LT Museum*

Car 1444 was completely rebuilt by the LCC in 1932. Originally a single truck M class vehicle, it received new bodywork and standard eight wheel, maximum traction trucks. It was reclassified ME/3 and, after being damaged in an accident, it was refurbished with a domed roof in October 1934. *LT Museum*

Car 1370 was reconditioned in July 1933 and reclassified ME/3. As such, it formed part of a class of three vehicles, which included cars 1441 and 1444. It is seen working special service 72X at the corner of Brockley Rise and Stondon Park. *D.A.Thompson/LCCT Trust*

The 100 series HR/2 vehicles came on the road in 1931. They lacked trolley poles, thus restricting them to conduit only routes. Members of this class were equipped with four motors and were primarily used for their hill climbing abilities. Car 122 is the lead vehicle in this picture of no less than five HR/2 trams. Car 1893 is a war damaged vehicle with a replacement top deck, car 1880 is a standard car of the 1930 batch of vehicles and car 1890 in the distance was reconstructed in December 1936. All this activity is taking place at Champion Park curve, Denmark Hill on 22nd September 1951. *J.H.Meredith*

HR/2 trolleyless car 111 is accelerating over the junction at Camberwell Green. According to the indicator blind it is on a short working to Lewisham Clock Tower. Lacking the necessary equipment for overhead wire equipped routes, this vehicle was scrapped in December 1951. The busy corridor from the Elephant & Castle to this point was at the time planned for a Bakerloo line extension that did not proceed, leaving the connection to be handled by a heavy presence of buses. *A.J. Watkins*

The white painted fender and the headlamp mask indicate that wartime blackout restrictions are in force. HR/2 class car 155 is pictured in Highgate Village, days before route 11 was abandoned on 10th December 1939. The presence of the policeman on the corner by the new trolleybus terminus is a reminder that any photographer out and about with his camera could be asked to prove his identity, in order to allay suspicions of spying for the enemy!

Car 156 is pictured in the appropriately named Short Street at the Elephant and Castle. Likely to cause apoplexy for other road users, this one way street was traversed by trams in the opposite direction to the prevailing traffic flow! This scene vanished completely when the area at the northern end of Walworth Road was later redeveloped.
D.A.Thompson/LCCT Trust

At Effra Road change pit car 1862 is in the process of shooting its plough. This referred to the swift ejection of the conduit plough from the underside of the car. The tram is already moving forward after taking power from the overhead. Change pit attendants made redundant by the conversion programme were found other jobs in the LT organisation.
J.H.Meredith

HR/2 class car 1866 passes the entrance to the depot at Camberwell Green. The equal wheel trucks typical of this class can clearly be seen. The HIGGS & HILL builders' notice is a sure indication that the structure is about to be demolished. Originally constructed for horse trams in 1871, the new bus garage, named Walworth, opened for business in October 1951. *J.H.Meredith*

The four track layout on Dog Kennel Hill was probably the most famous section of the London tramways. No two cars could ascend or descend on the same track. This was a safety arrangement designed to minimise the danger of a runaway vehicle careering into another. Car 1866 is about to make the climb. *J.Bonell/LCCT Trust*

At Blackwall Tunnel terminus car 1871 pulls away on the first leg of its journey to Victoria. The buildings, the small shops and the row of London plane trees were later replaced by the new approach road to the tunnel. The motorman of this tram proves the fact that London Transport's eyesight policy had been relaxed for those wearing glasses. *J.H.Meredith*

A light mist or heat haze envelops Camberwell Green on 29th September 1951. Car 1879 is about to pass a line of taxis stationed in the middle of the carriageway. Ahead is E/3 car 1995 heading for the City terminus at the northern end of Southwark Bridge. *J.H.Meredith*

Lewisham High Street was a busy place in tram days. Rehab car 1885 was renovated in November 1936 and was one of only six HR/2 vehicles to be so treated. The Salisbury was a well known local hostelry, where shoppers and market traders could slake their thirsts. Lewisham town centre is another area of the metropolis which has been 'modernised' by town planners and highways' engineers. *R.Hubble/LCCT Trust*

Roy Hubble tracked car 1885 northwards and caught up with it again in Tunnel Avenue by Greenfell Street. The large gas holders of the South Metropolitan Gas Works dominated the scene here for many years. With exception of one gas holder all was later swept away for the dual carriageway Blackwall Tunnel southern approach road and the North Greenwich Arena complex. *R.Hubble/LCCT Trust*

Car 1885 approaches the Red Lion, Walworth Road on its journey towards the Elephant and Castle. This vehicle was put to the scrapper's torch in May 1952. Away from the tram this area appears to have suffered less from the recent wartime bombing. There is still a wide variety of architectural styles in this busy South London thoroughfare.
D.A.Thompson/LCCT Trust

HR/2 rehab car 1887 is seen entering the single track by Barth Road, Plumstead. Electric traction predominated with trams and trolleybuses sharing the road space. This vehicle is nearing the end of its career. Like many other members of the HR/2 class it is working out its last days on the Woolwich and Eltham routes away from its original stamping ground of the Dulwich hills. *D.A.Thompson/LCCT Trust*

Opposite The E/3 class dated from 1930 and were similar in appearance to the HR/2 class, but were less powerful, only possessing two motors and riding on maximum traction trucks. Car 1905 is pictured at Streatham change pit. On the other side of the road a standard RT type bus heads for West Hampstead on route 59. This type of vehicle will soon be running on tram route replacement service 109 to Croydon and Purley.

18
CROYDON
PURLEY
1905
59
KEEP
LEFT
Procea
BREAD
LUC
85
GPB 700
BANK
MIDLAND B

Trafalgar Road, Greenwich is the location for car 1912 as it approaches the crossover by the William the Fourth public house. The tower of Christ Church rises just beyond the tram. It was at this spot that the standard gauge LCC conduit electric lines once met the narrow gauge tracks of the Woolwich & South East London horse tramway. *D.A.Thompson/LCCT Trust*

The Kentish Drovers Inn, Peckham High Street provides the background for car 1915. The date is 28th June 1952 and this E/3 class vehicle is approaching its last week of operation. Tram route 72 formed part of the final stage of 'Operation Tramaway' – the none too subtle official code word for the post-war conversion scheme. *J.C.Gillham*

The Lavender Hill Mob was a very popular British comedy of the early 1950s. Here on Lavender Hill, Battersea, near Clapham Junction Station, two years before the 1951 film made a name for the place, car 1927 nears the terminus. The rear blind has already been changed for the return journey. *J.H.Meredith*

26
BORO & LONDON
VIA WESTMINSTER
1927
Thorpes
BASS
ON DRAUGHT
Why wait until the General Election?
VOTE IN YOUR LOCAL ELECTIONS AND
Wise National Housekeeping by THE CONSERVATIVES
FAIRY

The Livesey Institute, Old Kent Road, was named after gas magnate, George Livesey. E/3 car 1937 has just crossed the bridge over the Surrey Canal, which opened in 1807 and was finally abandoned in the 1970s. The lone concrete bus stop minus its flag indicates that preparations are in hand for the end of the trams at this location. *D.A.Thompson/LCCT Trust*

Readers can make up their own minds as to the aesthetic qualities of trolleybus overhead wires vis-à-vis the LCC conduit tram tracks. During the pre-war tramway abandonment programme the 'intrusion' of new trolleybus overhead caused significant adverse comment from local residents. E/3 car 1941 and ex Leyton E/3 car 173 occupy Green Lanes by Clissold Park. Note the complete lack of other traffic. *D.A.Thompson/LCCT Trust*

Service 35 passed through the famous Kingsway Subway to terminate outside Highgate Archway Station. Car 1946 will shortly rumble over the crossover on the return trip to New Cross and Forest Hill. The journey was timed at 85 minutes and the through adult fare was one shilling and threepence (6p). *R.Hubble/LCCT Trust*

Opposite Essex Road tube station car 1948 passes the Three Brewers public house. This is the junction with Canonbury Road and New North Road. Here former tram route 11 once crossed route 33 at right angles. Remains of the connecting curve can be seen just in front of the tram. Note the war damaged buildings on the left of the picture. They have been buttressed against further collapse. *D.A.Thompson/LCCT Trust*

The Kingsway Subway was closed on 5th April 1952. Tram enthusiasts deemed this act the 'the crowning folly' of the tramway abandonment programme. An E/3 car is depicted here on the ramp leading to surface tracks on Southampton Row. This 1 in 10 gradient (10%) called for some skill from motormen, who had to make sure their charges did not roll back into Holborn Tram Station. *F.G. Reynolds*

In the days before plastic traffic cones roadworks were protected by oil lamps, wooden poles and red flags. Workmen appear to have vacated the scene outside Holloway Road tube station, as car 1981 loads passengers for the journey through the Kingsway Subway. Many Londoners, apprehensive about the claustrophobic atmosphere of the tube, would use the trams to go from north to south. Obviously the less enclosed nature of the Kingsway Subway and the two tram stations did not cause them discomfort. *D.A.Thompson/LCCT Trust*

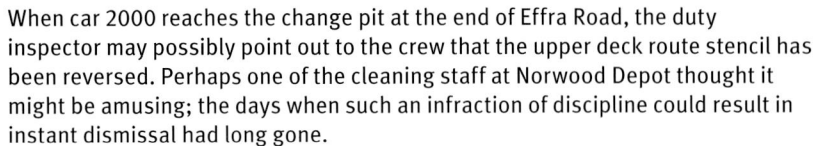

When car 2000 reaches the change pit at the end of Effra Road, the duty inspector may possibly point out to the crew that the upper deck route stencil has been reversed. Perhaps one of the cleaning staff at Norwood Depot thought it might be amusing; the days when such an infraction of discipline could result in instant dismissal had long gone.

The Kingsway Subway was a transport innovation years ahead of its time. It allowed trams to dive under surface traffic in central London. Here at Holborn Tram Station we look north towards the ramp leading to Southampton Row. The replacing buses were unable to use the subway and it fell into disuse. The southern section between the Embankment and Aldwych Tram Station has since been employed as an underpass for motor traffic. *A.B.Cross*

E/3 class car 2001 passes the entrance to Norwood Depot on 18th June 1950. The line of buses parked in the depot yard have been expelled from Norwood Garage on Knight's Hill. This sight was not a portent of things to come, because the tram depot was later sold by London Transport. It was considered unsuitable for diesel buses. *J.H.Meredith*

EPILOGUE – ABANDONMENT by Ken Blacker

When I set out from home with the express purpose of riding on London's last tram, it was as a semi-seasoned 'last nighter'. I had participated in a number of previous last nights and this was to be the climax of them all. Trams had been part of my life since my earliest years. I well remember, when travelling home on the upstairs of a tram, my father pointing out as we climbed the hill past Wood Green depot: "Those are the new electric buses in there". Trolleybuses were due to take the road on 8th May 1938 and I would have been aged just three. Later, as children, a much favoured cheap day out could be had by catching a 33 tram from Manor House to the Embankment, knowing that the climax of the journey would be a thrilling plunge into the dark depths of the Kingsway Subway.

The post-war tram conversion programme was part way through when I decided that, upon reaching the advanced age of sixteen and having just been taken on as a junior clerk by London Transport, I would take an active part in the remaining conversion stages. This meant deducing from the 'Red Book' - London Transport's internal working timetable - the last scheduled car on each conversion and travelling on it, followed by a few hours hanging around the streets before catching the first replacement bus en route to home. I missed the first few stages, but joined in at stage 5 on the Saturday night of 6th October 1951 when I and a few other last night 'regulars', some of whom are still on the enthusiast scene today, comprised the majority of passengers on the otherwise almost empty last tram through East Dulwich and up the steep, four track Dog Kennel Hill. The last car from Grove Park at stage 6 on 6th January 1952 was similarly sparsely attended, but in stark contrast, the final run through the Kingsway Subway on 6th April 1952 was jam packed. A trivial memory of that night was that the last car, E3 no. 185, had a pronounced 'flat' on one of its wheels which meant that you could recognise its approach from some distance away.

Kingsway Subway was the penultimate conversion and it left only the network of routes based on New Cross and Abbey Wood depots still to fall. At the time I was ambivalent as to whether the conversion to buses was a good thing or not. Without doubt the remaining trams were horribly outdated. In terms of passenger comfort they ranked far below the LT and ST motor buses that I had grown used to travelling on to school each day (and which had all but vanished by the end of 1949), and in terms of accessibility their difficult platform steps and ridiculous staircases were an indictment of the London County Council's retrograde design policy of the early nineteen-thirties. On the other hand, I had seen in the Underground group's splendid Feltham cars the sheer untapped potential of what a modern tram could embody, and to this day I still believe that these were the most advanced passenger road vehicles for their time ever to enter London service. However the Felthams had all gone to pastures new in Leeds by the time I began my last night jaunts, and apart from the ornately decorated, highly varnished wooden lower deck ceilings on some of the ex-municipal cars at Abbey Wood, there was not much to be recommended about the remaining London tram fleet.

And so we came to the last day, and then the last night. After several hours of final joy riding by tram our little group of last-nighters rode out to Woolwich to get favourably positioned for our last 'last ride' by London tram, all of us knowing that this would be a more special occasion than any of the others. Very many years have passed since then and I have been on many 'lasts' in many places. The feeling has always been the same, a strange mixture of excitement at participating in the making of transport history, and of inevitable sadness – disbelief almost – that a feature of life I had taken for granted over the years would be gone for ever. There is nothing more final than riding along on a tram, trolleybus or whatever, knowing that another one will never pass that way again. But the end of Britain's greatest tramway network on 5th July 1952 was something extra special, and I was aware of this as I positioned myself at the head of the queue at Perrott Street, Woolwich, for the route 40 tram departure scheduled at 11.56pm to New Cross depot where a big closing ceremony was planned when it arrived there at 12.26am.

Perrott Street is one of those undistinguished side turnings that you would never notice in normal times, and it only came to fame because of the crossing here, in Plumstead Road, that marked the off-peak outer terminus of route 40. We arrived there with almost two hours to spare, and in plenty of time to observe the last comings and goings on routes 36/38 and 40. In normal times we would also have seen the running-in journeys on routes 44 and 46 to Abbey Wood depot but tonight they were absent, having been diverted from their terminus at Beresford Square direct to the scrapyard. A substantial queue built up behind us, well in excess of what any 74-seat E3 could ever hope to accommodate. The evening drew on, and the last 36/38 came up from Abbey Wood, to the best of my recollection more or less on schedule at 11.43. And then it was time for what was scheduled to be the last car of all.

No. 1951 duly turned up to start its final run to New Cross, and to my surprise the lower deck already appeared to be half full of what I took to be BBC sound recordists and their gear. Space for ordinary passengers was obviously going to be more restricted than I had originally imagined. Worse still, the driver overshot the Perrott Street stop by a considerable distance, which mean that everyone at the back of the queue boarded first in what became a veritable scrum. The others in our little group managed to elbow their way on, but I obviously didn't push hard enough as I was left stranded on the pavement at Perrott Street as the car pulled away. In a mild degree of panic I ran as fast as I could behind it hoping that, if I could catch it up at Beresford Square – two minutes' journey time away – it was likely to be delayed there and I might be able to get on. It was, indeed, delayed for quite a while at Beresford Square, but so huge was the crowd that I was unable to get anywhere near it.

Just as I was becoming gripped by despair at missing London's last tram despite all my best efforts, the totally unexpected happened. From the direction of Grand Depot Road came a number 72 tram which circled the Beresford Square loop and parked up at the normal 72 departure stop in New Road with its destination blinds clearly showing 'New Cross Gate'. At first few people seemed to notice it, the great majority being preoccupied with no. 1951. I had no idea why it was here, for the last 72 was scheduled to have departed at 11.31, but I immediately seized the opportunity and was one of

On 5th July 1952 farewell tours were organised over the remaining routes. On Westhorne Avenue, Eltham a multitude of tram enthusiasts and their families have occupied the roadway. This was truly a unique occasion. One wonders how all this lot managed to fit on just two trams, but the system showed right up to the bitter end that it was more than capable of moving large numbers of people safely.

the first to board no. 187, claiming a premium seat upstairs at the front. The tram filled, gradually at first and then more rapidly almost to overflowing, but the crew seemed to be in no hurry to depart. As we sat motionless at the stop, 1951 made its way out of Beresford Square at about ten minutes after midnight and I knew, there and then, that we would inevitably get to New Cross Gate after the official last tram. Even if we had departed immediately and maintained a good road speed, the circuitous 72 routing via Lee and Lewisham required nine minutes more running time than the direct, 'lower' road through Charlton and Greenwich. The crew of 187 would have known this too, but they were obviously pursuing their own last tram night agenda, and when we finally set off no attempt was made to correct the late running and much of the journey was at little more than ambling pace.

Of the journey itself, there is nothing much to report. The car gradually emptied as passengers alighted, but not before a collecting hat had been passed around for the crew, to which I very gladly contributed. No trams passed going the other way and as far as I was aware we were the only tramcar still on this lengthy section of track. A few bystanders waved as we went past, notably souvenir hunters began removing bits and pieces which I didn't really approve of, illogically really since 187 was destined to go for scrap anyway. Although what possible use tramcar light bulbs would have been to anybody is hard to imagine! For the last time I witnessed a change pit in action as we moved from the overhead supply to the conduit at Lee Green. The centre of Lewisham – which I had already visited twice late at night in recent months for the last 58 and then the last 54 – was largely deserted. For some reason, it struck me as particularly strange to think that, though the

rails were still glistening, there would be no trams in Lewisham any more. Finally, as we drifted down Lewisham Way towards New Cross, we began to pass little groups of people walking the other way, who I assumed were making their way home after witnessing the Last Tram ceremony. I wondered what they made of it all as our tram passed by.

To the best of my recollection we reached journey's end at New Cross Gate at about 1.30am where we found a sizeable number of bystanders still milling around. Lord Latham had already given his famous "Farewell Old Tram" oration on the slope up to the depot, and I had missed all of that. I presumed that many in the crowd were hanging about in the hope of seeing New Cross depot empty as the last few cars departed, out of service, for the tram graveyard at Penhall Road. I was the last passenger to alight from 187 and for me this truly marked the end of an era. And from a purely personal perspective, the fact that my last ride had been on an E3 was a particular bonus, as throughout my life this was the class of car that I had known best of all. 187 didn't go into New Cross depot, but reversed outside and was taken straight away unceremoniously to the scrapyard. I watched it go and never saw it again.

As a postscript, I have heard in very recent times that another car – from Abbey Wood depot – may also have been out late at night and could, in fact, have been London's very last service tram. If so, I never saw it and can only assume it was somewhere in the Eltham area which my 72 bypassed by taking the short cut via Westhorne Avenue. If there were any enthusiasts on it I hope that they will always treasure, as I do, their poignant memories of London's last tram night.

In this classic scene the conductor of a short working service 40 car changes the points in Lewisham Way. On 5th July 1952 the service was more than a little disrupted by the large numbers of last day riders. Many tram crews found themselves having to use common sense in order to keep things ticking over. There was no extra rolling stock available, as for some bizarre reason London Transport had been withdrawing trams in the final week. Note the sandbag positioned on the driver's cab roof to prevent ingress of rain water. *W.J. Wyse*

The crowds of those wishing to have one last ride increased towards midday on Saturday, 5th July 1952. London Transport inspectors were out in force in an attempt to marshal the large numbers of people who had made their way to the Victoria Embankment. Car 1908 with a reversed 40 stencil is about to set off on its journey to Woolwich. Souvenir tickets were issued for the Last Week and these soon became collectors' items. *W.J. Wyse*

We witness a suitably staged scene for the last day of London's trams, 5th July 1952. Fine summer weather has brought out sightseers, well wishers, nostalgia enthusiasts and photographers in their droves. Here on the Embankment a conductor poses in front of a phalanx of cameras. *LT Museum*

Former Walthamstow car 2055 is depicted outside Charlton Works on the last night. Someone inside the works has 'doctored' the LAST TRAM WEEK poster on the side of the tram. Charlton Works outlived the trams and finally closed in 1959. Less than a month after this picture was taken, car 2055 had been scrapped at Penhall Road Yard. *LT Museum*

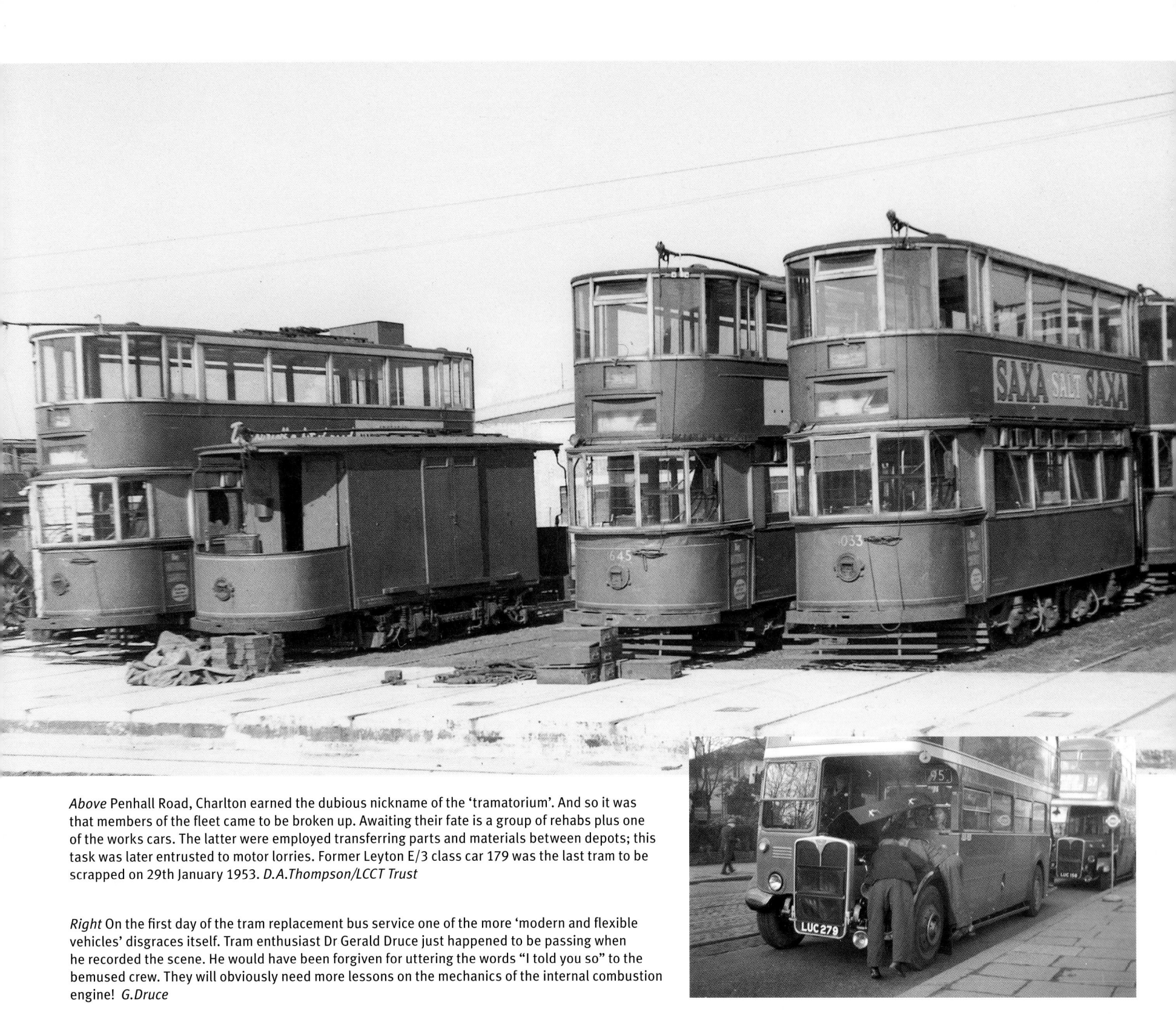

Above Penhall Road, Charlton earned the dubious nickname of the 'tramatorium'. And so it was that members of the fleet came to be broken up. Awaiting their fate is a group of rehabs plus one of the works cars. The latter were employed transferring parts and materials between depots; this task was later entrusted to motor lorries. Former Leyton E/3 class car 179 was the last tram to be scrapped on 29th January 1953. *D.A.Thompson/LCCT Trust*

Right On the first day of the tram replacement bus service one of the more 'modern and flexible vehicles' disgraces itself. Tram enthusiast Dr Gerald Druce just happened to be passing when he recorded the scene. He would have been forgiven for uttering the words "I told you so" to the bemused crew. They will obviously need more lessons on the mechanics of the internal combustion engine! *G.Druce*

96